Praise for *The Difference Maker*

"God loves to use everyday, ordinary people to make a difference. Jesus demonstrated that with Peter when he invited him to follow and learn to be a fisher of men. Nelson lays out in *The Difference Maker* a simple, yet profound process to impact others for eternity."

—*Jeff Newman*, Senior Pastor,
The Austin Vineyard, Austin, TX

"Our #1 job as developing followers of Jesus, according to The Great Commission, is to go and make disciples. In your hands you hold, not only the job description, but the detailed strategy to get it done."

—*Stan Pegram,* Lead Pastor,
BMZ Church, Boscobel, WI

"Many sincere and loving Christians want to reach out with the Good News of Jesus Christ, but they can't seem to take the first and second steps. In a brief, yet powerful book, Nelson demystifies and gives practical systematic steps to help others move towards Christ and His Church."

—*Rev. Alan Howe*, Senior Pastor,
Eden United Methodist Church, Eden, NY

"I am looking forward to using *The Difference Maker* as a powerful tool to motivate and mobilize an army of Great Commission 'difference makers' here."

—**Robert Haynes**, Senior Pastor,
New Life Community Church, Olive Branch, MS

"*The Difference Maker* is a real solution to one of the greatest fears gripping Christianity and that's making an eternal impact in the lives of others. Nelson simply reveals how to leverage your influence to offer something that everyone enjoys getting and that's an invitation to be included."

—**Scott Reynolds**, Lead Pastor,
North River Church, Tuscaloosa, AL
Author of *Journey Deeper*

"If you want a quick read that motivates you to share your faith, *The Difference Maker* is the one! Envelop these time-tested principles of life practice into your spiritual maturity."

—**Dr. David Miracle**, Lead Pastor,
Watershed, San Antonio, TX

"Nelson Searcy does it again by taking the basic beliefs of the faith that every believer needs to not only know, but do and presents them in simple action steps that any person can understand and make a part of their life. *The Difference Maker* is the book for pastors to give to every member in preparation of a big day like Easter or a new series."

—***Roger House***, Lead Pastor,
Allen Street Baptist, Clinton, MO

"I've known Nelson a long time and what he shares here is right on target and will help church members get out of their comfort zone and be true Difference Makers in sharing their faith. It's powerful stuff that every Christian should embrace!"

—***Jimmy Britt,*** Senior Pastor
Rocky River Church, Concord NC

the
difference
maker

the difference maker

Using Your Everyday Life for Eternal Impact

nelson searcy

with jennifer dykes henson

Library of Congress Cataloging-in-Publication Data

Searcy, Nelson

The difference maker : using your everyday life for eternal impact/ Nelson Searcy with Jennifer Dykes Henson.

p. cm.

Includes bibliographical references.

ISBN 978-0-9885241-5-6

1. Religion—Christian Life—Spiritual Growth

contents

introduction:
becoming a difference maker

I know it's scary. Even though you realize you should—and deep down you want to—there's something about talking to others about Jesus that makes you clam up. You're afraid of what they'll think. You're afraid they have negative perceptions of Christians and that they'll project those perceptions onto you. You're afraid they may think you're crazy, that they'll whisper behind your back. Or that they'll pull away from the relationship because they think you are trying to "convert" them.

The enemy uses these whispers and lies to keep you from making a difference in the world. But when you step back and shine the light of truth on his deceit, you come to realize that making a difference isn't that hard, after all. There's nothing to be scared of. In fact, God has uniquely positioned you to influence the people in your life for him. And he has only one requirement you have to meet in order to qualify. You simply have to be open to using your everyday life for eternal impact. In other words, you have to be willing to be a Difference Maker.

In the pages ahead, we are going to uncover a number of ways you can make a difference in the lives of those around you. We're going to discover the power of your personal story and how God can use it to transform others (chapters 2 and 3). We're going to examine what it means to be ready to be used by God, no matter where you are or who you're with (chapter 4). We're going to study some illustrations that will help you talk about the fine points of your faith without feeling intimidated (chapters 5 through 8). In short, we're going to explore the ins-and-outs of what it means to be a Difference Maker for Jesus right where he has placed you.

But before we dive into those finer points, we'll begin by discovering the single easiest way to make a difference (chapter 1). Becoming a Difference Maker isn't as difficult as you may think. Even before you know how to tell your story effectively or walk someone through detailed discussions about Christianity, God can use you. God wants to use you. *You.* Not your neighbor, your spouse or your more articulate friend. *You.* He wants to partner with you in changing people's lives both now and for eternity. To start being used by God, all you need is a heart turned toward those around you who don't know Jesus and a willingness to offer them one eternity-changing invitation. What exactly is that invitation? Read on.

1

the easiest way to make
a difference

But my life is worth nothing to me unless I use it for finishing the work assigned me by the Lord Jesus—the work of telling others the Good News about the wonderful grace of God.

Apostle Paul (Acts 20:24)

How many weddings have you been invited to? How many graduations? Birthday bashes? Baby showers? House-warming parties? How many times have you been asked by a friend or family member to grab dinner or go to a movie? Do you ever get invited to dance recitals or soccer games for your friends' kids? Cookouts or pool parties on hot summer days? Christmas get-togethers? New Year's celebrations?

You and I live in a culture that swaps invitations freely. Over the course of a year, you probably receive hundreds of them. So do most people you know. Given this reality, it's good that invitations are always positive, even flattering. Whether it's for a significant life event or just out for ice cream, an invitation means that someone thinks enough of you to include you. They want to spend time with you and share an experience. An invitation places instant value on your presence and speaks to your esteem in the life of the one who has extended it. And whether or not you want to attend what you've been invited to, I bet you're usually happy to have been thought of, right?

An Eternity-Changing Invitation

Even though our lives are filled with invitations big and small, ironically, the most important invitation we can offer someone is often the hardest to extend. It's an invitation that can impact the course of someone's life in the present and change his or her eternity. It can lead to a new relationship that will infuse love, hope and purpose into the darkest of circumstances and bring added joy to all that's already good. Still, we hesitate. We hedge. We are slow to ask the one simple question that can have incredible implications for the invitee: *Would you like to come to church with me this weekend?*

Inviting someone to church isn't complicated. It doesn't require you to know the Bible from cover to cover. You don't have to be able to outline the life and ministry of Jesus, or offer proof of his deity. You don't have to engage in conversations about grace and redemption (though over time and through the help of these pages you may get to the point where you are comfortable doing just that). No, all it takes is the willingness to offer a simple invitation.

Inviting someone to church doesn't have to be scary or intimidating, either. You and I have a tendency to make it so by choosing the wrong perspective. Instead of focusing on what the invitation might mean for the person we're inviting, we focus on ourselves. I understand how it is. You build up the scenario in your mind and reinforce it with negative hypothetical scaffolding. You think about all of the questions they could ask you that you wouldn't know the answer to. You worry what they'll think of you. You make a mental list of all the things that could go wrong.

But none of these mental charades are rooted in truth.

Contrary to the fears that try to creep in and keep you silent, research shows that your friends and family members will likely respond positively when you offer them an invitation to church. Study after study reports that fifty percent of those you invite will join you for a

service the first time you ask. Another twenty-five percent will come when offered a second or third invitation. So seventy-five percent of the people you invite to
church will say yes. And the other twenty-five percent
will appreciate the thought and effort of your invitation
even if they decline it.[1]

Fortunately, people have been sidestepping their hesitation and offering invitations for others to come with them
to meet Jesus since he first began his ministry over two
thousand years ago. Jesus' apostle, John, records two such
invitations that ended up changing the course of history:

> *Andrew, Simon Peter's brother, was one of these men
> who heard what John said and then followed Jesus.
> Andrew went to find his brother, Simon, and told
> him, 'We have found the Messiah' (which means
> 'Christ'). Then **Andrew brought Simon to meet
> Jesus**. Looking intently at Simon, Jesus said, 'Your
> name is Simon, son of John—but you will be called
> Cephas' (which means 'Peter').*
>
> *The next day Jesus decided to go to Galilee. He
> found Philip and said to him, 'Come, follow me.'
> Philip was from Bethsaida, Andrew and Peter's
> hometown. Philip went to look for Nathanael and
> told him, 'We have found the very person Moses and*

the prophets wrote about! His name is Jesus, the son of Joseph from Nazareth.'

'Nazareth!' exclaimed Nathanael. 'Can anything good come from Nazareth?'

'Come and see for yourself,' *Philip replied.*

As they approached, Jesus said, 'Now here is a genuine son of Israel—a man of complete integrity.'

'How do you know about me?' Nathanael asked.

Jesus replied, 'I could see you under the fig tree before Philip found you.'

Then Nathanael exclaimed, 'Rabbi, you are the Son of God—the King of Israel!'

(John 1:40-48, emphasis added)

Andrew couldn't have had any idea what God had in store for his brother when he brought him to meet Jesus. But thankfully, Andrew was eager to offer an invitation and Peter was quick to accept. After coming face-to-face with Jesus, Peter's life changed completely. He went on to lead the early church and turn the known world upside down.

Your invitation can make an eternal difference in the lives of the people God has put around you.

Nathanael, on the other hand, was a little more skeptical when Philip approached him about Jesus. He pushed back. He questioned whether or not Jesus' claims could be legitimate. But Philip didn't take Nathanael's cynicism personally. He simply responded, "Come and see for yourself!" Nathanael did, and one brief encounter with Jesus convinced Nathanael that he had met the Messiah.

These two great men of God may never have come to know Jesus if Andrew and Philip hadn't been willing to offer an invitation. Peter may have never heard about Jesus from someone he trusted if Andrew hadn't stepped up. Nathanael may never have become a follower if Phillip hadn't challenged him to look into Jesus for himself. Likewise, there are people in your life who will never have a real encounter with Jesus unless you take the initiative to offer them an invitation to church.

Four Keys to a Powerful Invitation

Never underestimate the power of your invitation. God can and will work through it to make an eternal difference in the lives of the people he has put around you. But before you are ready to be used by God to invite others to church, four key things have to happen. You must:

1. Believe that Jesus can change lives.
2. Recognize that God wants to use you.
3. Identify the people God wants you to invite to church.
4. Care enough to extend an invitation.

Let's look at each one of these in more detail.

1. Believe that Jesus can change lives.

How has Jesus changed your life? Think about how he has forgiven you, brought you out of your sin and given you a new destiny. Consider what he is teaching you now. Think about the peace that his promise of an eternity with him in heaven brings.

When you spend time thinking through just how much Jesus has transformed your own life, you will begin to burn with a desire to share his good news with other people. You'll want others to know him the way you do, to find hope and security in his goodness. None of us who love our friends and family members want them to die apart from Jesus. We want them to know him because we understand that he will not only make a difference in their eternity (2 Timothy 1:10), but he will also bring joy and purpose to their everyday lives in the present (Matthew 11:28).

Do you really believe that your friend's life would be better if she knew Jesus? Do you believe that the person next to you at work or your neighbor around the cul-de-sac would benefit from experiencing God's love on a personal level? If you do, then you owe it to those individuals to offer an invitation to join you at church. Invite them to come and see for themselves what Jesus is all about. You are the catalyst God wants to use in their lives.

2. Recognize that God wants to use you.

When God entered your life and brought you to a saving knowledge of himself, he knew you had great potential. After all, he is the one who gave you that potential. Now, he wants to tap into it. He wants to use you to help him do his work. Can you imagine anything better than partnering with God to fulfill his purposes in this world?

No matter what stage of life you are in, where you live, where you work, where you go to school, or who your friends are, God has placed you exactly where you are for a specific reason. It's no coincidence that you have a good rapport with that unchurched workmate in your office. It's no coincidence that your unbelieving cousin has more respect for you and your opinion than he does for many others in his life. That's where influence begins—the influence God wants you to use to point people in his direction.

God has uniquely positioned you to have immense impact. You're the one he wants to use in your circles of influence. If the people around you don't hear about Jesus from you, they may never hear about him in a way that resonates with them. Just like Andrew was the one who cared enough to invite Peter to see Jesus; just like Philip was the one able to challenge Nathanael to learn about Jesus for himself; there are people who have been intentionally placed in proximity to you so they can hear about Jesus from you. God has set the stage for you to be the Difference Maker in their lives. He is calling you to be open to using your life to impact theirs.

3. Identify the people God wants you to invite to church.

Once you understand that Jesus wants to use you in the lives of those around you, you have to get practical about exactly who he wants you to reach out to. Begin by considering your sphere of influence. These are the people God has positioned you to influence most effectively:

- *Family*: Is there someone in your family with a misguided idea of who Jesus is, someone who needs to be introduced to him in a true and thoughtful way? Is there a family member whose need for God is weighing on your heart?

- *Friends*: Who do you interact with socially? Do they know Jesus? Are they struggling to understand what a relationship with God is all about? Are they going through difficult life circumstances?

- *Coworkers/Classmates*: Your friends and your coworkers (or classmates, if you are in school) may overlap, but I bet there are also many you don't know very well at all. You may see them around and even know them by name, but the relationship has never moved beyond acquaintance status. Who among these people is God putting on your heart? Who do you think may be open to an invitation to church? Be careful not to say no for them. You have no idea how God is working to prepare them for your invitation.

- *Neighbors*: Do you always seem to run into the same person around the neighborhood or at the gym? Maybe it's the guy you see at the drycleaners or the woman whose child is in the same gymnastics class as yours. God has positioned you in your neighbors' lives to talk about more than just the weather. Be willing to engage a real conversation—one that could lead to the opportunity to extend an invitation.

No doubt, God has brought family members, friends, coworkers or classmates and neighbors to your mind. Let me challenge you to grab a pen and write their names down here:

1. _____

2. _____

3. _____

4. _____

5. _____

6. _____

7. _____

8. _____

9. _____

10. _____

You are uniquely positioned to have a voice with these individuals. Thank God for that. Then, pray he will give you just the right opportunity to reach out. When that opportunity shows itself, make the most of it. As Paul wrote:

> *Live wisely among those who are not believers, and make the most of every opportunity.* (Colossians 4:5)

4. Care enough to extend an invitation.

When you really believe that Jesus can change lives, that he wants to use you, and that he has put people in your path specifically for you to influence for him, then there's only one thing you can do in response: care enough to extend the all-important invitation. Ask, *Would you like to come to church with me?*

Don't make it harder than it has to be.

The number one reason people attend church for the first time—that is, the number one reason people step into an environment where they can hear the truth about Jesus proclaimed—is because someone they respect invited them. Be that someone. Again, half of those you ask will come to church with you the very first time you ask them. To increase the percentage even more, try inviting them out to breakfast before church or to lunch after. Planning a casual meal around the service often gives hesitant first-timers a little more incentive.

No matter what approach you take, be intentional about dismissing your negative thoughts. Focus on what the invitation could mean for the person you are inviting, rather than on your own unfounded fears. God has called you to this. The people you are inviting will be happy you care enough about them to offer an invitation. Don't make it harder than it has to be.

The Best Time for an Invitation

While any weekend is a good weekend for an unchurched friend or family member to join you at church, there are certain times during the year you may find it easier to make the ask—and when the person you are inviting may be more open than usual to saying *yes*:

- *Easter*—Easter provides you with an incredible opportunity to invite someone to church with you. Most people on your list will join you without hesitation for an Easter service. Plus, this is a great time to extend an invitation to those hard cases in your life—the ones who would likely fall into the twenty-five percent who would decline your offer any other time of year.

- *A Big Day*—A *Big Day* in your church is simply a special service that gives you a unique chance to invite a friend. Maybe your pastor is kicking off a brand new teaching series or a guest speaker is coming in to discuss an interesting topic. These out-of-the-ordinary opportunities that are naturally built into your church's annual calendar give you even more leverage when offering an invitation to the people in your sphere of influence.

- *Topic-Specific Messages*—When you know in advance what your pastor will be teaching on in the weeks to come, it gives you the opportunity to invite people who may relate specifically to those topics. For example, if you know an upcoming message will be about restoring broken relationships, you can use that as an opportunity to invite someone in your life who is struggling with a troubled marriage or a distant child. Or if the message is going to be on lowering stress and finding peace, you can use it to entice your friend who constantly seems like she's at the end of her rope. Topic-specific messages let you target your invitations toward the right people at the right time.

That being said, each and every service at your church gives you a chance to be a Difference Maker. The special opportunities above simply support and enhance your ability to reach out to those around you effectively. Keep them in mind as you prepare to invite the people in your life into environments that may change their lives forever.

Making a Difference

God used Andrew and Philip's willingness to extend an invitation as a means to change the course of history. He wants to use you in the same way. He wants to partner with you in touching lives and making a difference in the world. The goal of the rest of this book is to give you the tools you need be a Difference Maker. That is, to equip you to live your everyday life in a way that will have an eternal impact. But you can go ahead and get started here and now, before you even turn another page. You are perfectly positioned and possess everything you need to begin making a difference in the world around you.

Nine little words: *Would you like to come to church with me?* By asking that question, you can become one of the greatest Difference Makers the world has ever known. Are you willing? Do you believe that Jesus can really change lives? Do you care enough to extend an invitation? As you begin inviting the people in your spheres of influence to church with you, not only will those you touch be forever grateful, but God will also grow you and bless you in ways you've never imagined.

2

a story to tell

I love to tell the story; For some have never heard.
The message of salvation. From God's own holy Word.

Katherine Hanky (Classic Hymn)

A good friend of mine once told me that he didn't
think his story of salvation would impact anyone.
In his opinion, it was boring. He had grown up in
church, had given his life to the Lord at a young age,
and had never strayed far from the straight and narrow.
As such, he felt like he hadn't been through anything
interesting enough to impact others for Jesus. I assured
him that the people I talk to who have the opposite
stories—stories of running from God, stories full of
mistakes and poor decisions—would love to hear his.

They would give anything to have lived it themselves, especially if it meant never having to go through so much of what it took to bring them to their knees.

I've also spent a lot of time with people on the other end of the spectrum, counseling those whose pasts are so sordid the details would make you blush. Many of them have stories filled with the pain of addictions, the pain of lost relationships, and the pain of regret. They think that what they've been through is too heavy to share with anyone else, and that others wouldn't be able to relate. But on the contrary, their stories of redemption—of finding God and the grace he offers after a lifetime of hardship—are often the most powerful.

No matter the details of your personal God story, it will resonate with the people who hear it. By their very nature, stories pique our interest. They cause us to sit up and take notice. Think about the last time you found your mind wandering while listening to a public speaker. Even if you had been tuning the person out for ten minutes, I bet you snapped back to attention when he or she started telling a personal story. Why? Because stories knock on our hearts in a way that makes us open the door, especially when they are stories about who God is and what he has done. By engaging us on an emotional level, these stories help us see new truths about the world around us and about ourselves.

While you and I are usually quick to dismiss our stories as uneventful, too eventful, or altogether unimportant, none of the above is true. If you are a follower of Jesus, you have a magnificent story to tell. That story is what God wants to use to show himself to the on-looking world. As author Shauna Niequist writes:

> There are two myths that we tend to believe about our stories: the first is that they're about us, and the second is that because they're about us, they don't matter. But they're not only about us, and they matter more than ever right now. When we, any of us who have been transformed by Christ, tell our own stories, we're telling the story of who God is.…
>
> There's nothing small or inconsequential about our stories. There is, in fact, nothing bigger. And when we tell the truth about our lives—the broken parts, the secret parts, the beautiful parts—then the gospel comes to life, an actual story about redemption, instead of abstraction and theory and things you learn in Sunday school.[2]

In Christian circles, we have another name for our stories. We call them *testimonies*. What's your testimony? Its key elements are already in place. There was a time when you didn't know Jesus. What did your life look like then? There was a series of events that led you to the place of being willing to turn your life over to him. What were they? There was a moment of conversion when you asked him to come into your life. How and when did that happen? And there's the ongoing story of how he has changed you and continues to change you as you walk with him every day.

God wants to use your story for his glory.

No matter what has or hasn't happened to you, where you come from or what your life looked like before Jesus intersected it, God wants to use every detail of your story for his glory. The tale of what he has done and is doing in your midst carries more power than you can imagine. There's no better way to connect with people and to make a difference in their lives than to share heartfelt truths about your own journey.

Three Essential Elements of Storytelling

As you begin to think about sharing your God story with others, there are three essential elements of good storytelling to keep in mind. First, you must confirm you have a story to tell. In other words, make sure you've had a true encounter with Jesus. Secondly, think through, and even write out, how you would tell your story to an interested listener. Remind yourself of the key moments, important characters and unexpected plot twists, so that you can tell your God story completely, clearly and powerfully. I like to call this *completing* your story. And finally, commit your story to God, knowing that he will use it to change lives as you share it with the people he has placed around you.

Let's examine each of these three storytelling elements in more detail:

1. Confirm Your Story

For Jesus to be able to use you as a Difference Maker, you first have to confirm your own encounter with him. When did you believe in Jesus Christ for the first time? What was going on in your life? Was it an intellectual decision or more emotional? Think about that moment. Confirm you've had it. You can't tell anyone else about Jesus' incredible gift of salvation if you have never experienced it for yourself.

The Apostle Paul described what it means to have a saving encounter with Jesus in his letter to the Romans:

> *If you openly declare that Jesus is Lord and believe in your heart that God raised him from the dead,*

you will be saved. For it is by believing in your heart that you are made right with God, and it is by openly declaring your faith that you are saved. (Romans 10:9-10)

Once you have believed in your heart and professed with your mouth that Jesus is the Son of God, you don't have to wonder whether or not you are saved. You can rest assured that you have a relationship with him and the promise of eternal life (1 John 5:13). If, for some reason, this book is in your hands but you have never asked Jesus into your life, let me encourage you to pray this prayer:

Dear God, I open my heart to you and invite you into my life. I confess that I am a sinner. I ask that you would forgive me of all that I've done wrong. Thank you for sending your Son, Jesus, who died for me and who gives me the opportunity to know you. From this moment on, I want to follow Jesus, in the fellowship of his church. Thank you for accepting me. In Jesus' name I pray. Amen.

If you just prayed that prayer for the first time, congratulations! Even though you may not understand all that it means right now, you have entered into a personal relationship with Jesus Christ. He has impacted your life with his grace and love. No matter what your past has been, good or bad, you have the hope of a new, better future in him. Be sure to tell your pastor about the decision you've made.

Now that you can confirm that you have had a true encounter with Jesus, you have a powerful story to tell.

2. Complete Your Story

Whether you became a Christian six minutes ago or sixty years ago, the best way to be ready to tell your story is to take the time to write it out. Think through the details of how God has shown himself to you and what he has done in your life. Reflect on and jot down the answers to these questions:

- *Your Life Before Christ*: Where were you spiritually before receiving Jesus? How did that affect your feelings, attitudes, actions and relationships? What caused you to begin thinking about accepting Jesus as your savior?

_____

_____

_____

_____

_____

_____

_____

_____

_____

_____

_____

- ***How You Came to Christ***: What realization did you come to that finally motivated you to ask Jesus to come into your life? Specifically, how did you receive Christ?

_____

_____

_____

_____

_____

_____

_____

_____

_____

_____

_____

- ***Your Life Since Becoming a Christian***:
  How has your life changed since you became
  a Christian? What benefits have you experienced as a result of entering into a relationship with Jesus?

_____

_____

_____

_____

_____

_____

_____

_____

_____

_____

Thinking through your journey to knowing God and writing down the specifics of how he has worked in your life will help you be prepared when he gives you the opportunity to share with someone. It's also a good idea to practice what you will say. Try telling your story to your spouse or to a trusted friend, just to get the hang of articulating the message you want to share.

As you tell your story, make sure to use simple words and be concise. Avoid saying things that could be considered religious cliché or "God-talk." That's like using an insider language that unbelievers can't fully understand. Also, try not to talk too much. You should be able to tell your story in about three minutes. Being direct and to-the-point goes a long way. (In the next chapter, we'll take a look at one of the most succinct, yet most powerful, testimonies ever given about God's goodness.) And remember, this isn't a script you have to follow verbatim. Just be yourself when you talk to people and emphasize aspects of your story that you think they'll be able to relate to best.

3. Commit Your Story to God

God has allowed you to walk the path you've walked for a reason. He has given you your story. Now, give it back to him. Commit it to him and ask him to use it to touch the family, friends, coworkers and neighbors he has intentionally positioned in your life.

Addressing the early church, the Apostle Paul wrote:

> *But my life is worth nothing to me unless I use it for finishing the work assigned me by the Lord Jesus— the work of telling others the Good News about the wonderful grace of God.* (Acts 20:24)

When you choose to step out of your comfort zone and share your story of redemption, it will make a difference every single time. God will use it mightily to shine his good news to others who are searching for peace, forgiveness, joy and a more abundant life.

My Story

Let me close this chapter by telling you my story:

43

When I turned seventeen years old, I was already working on an engineering degree at North Carolina State University, while traveling and speaking at various conferences for young entrepreneurs. Because I had started a successful computer business in high school, I ended up on this speaking circuit. At one of the conferences, I met a man who had written a book I wanted to read, so I headed to a local bookstore to pick it up. While I was browsing the shelves, I noticed a book by Billy Graham called *Peace With God*. I bought Dr. Graham's book on a whim, thinking it was a history book about a guy I had heard a little about while growing up in North Carolina.

So, in October of 1989, I was reading through *Peace With God* and got to the page where Billy Graham offered an invitation of salvation to any reader who didn't know Jesus. God convicted my heart. I prayed the prayer Dr. Graham had laid out for me there and then saw a toll-free number that he suggested I call.

I went back to my little apartment in Raleigh and called the 800 number. Yep, I'm that guy. The person on the other end encouraged me to do a few things—read my Bible, pray, get involved in a good church and make my decision public through baptism.

After I gave my life to God, he put me on a new path. I ended up getting my bachelor's degree in Religion and

Psychology at Gardner-Webb University and then a Masters of Divinity at Duke University, while pastoring a little church outside of Charlotte. Eventually, I moved to Southern California to work with Rick Warren and the Purpose Driven Community. Then in 2000, my wife, Kelley, and I moved to Manhattan to start The Journey Church of the City. In 2010, we moved to Boca Raton to lead The Journey Church of South Florida.

God came into my life that fall afternoon in Raleigh. He put me on a journey I never could have imagined—and I thank him for it every day. That's my story. What's yours? As Jesus' disciple Peter wrote:

> *...if someone asks about your hope as a believer, always be ready to explain it.* —1 Peter 3:15

If someone asks you why you believe in Jesus, are you prepared to answer?

Once you know you've had an encounter with God, taken a little time to complete the details of what he's done in your life, and committed your story to him—get ready. He will use it—and you—to make a difference for him right where he has placed you.

3

your story can change the world

Storytelling is the most powerful way to put ideas into the world today.

Robert McKee

God has given you a story to tell and that story can change the world. The catch is, you have to be ready and willing to tell it. Telling your story is an ordinary action that can have an eternal impact on the people around you. But like a gift that never gets opened, a story that never gets told can't serve the purpose it was meant for. If you don't tell others what God has done in your life, he can't use it to impact the world.

In the last chapter, we looked at some things to keep in mind as you share your story with the people in your spheres of influence:

- Use simple words.
- Be concise.
- Avoid religious clichés and God-talk.
- Keep your story to about three minutes.
- Be direct and to-the-point.

One of the greatest, simplest stories of God transforming a life is recorded in Scripture by Jesus' apostle, John. John penned the account of a man whose testimony checked all of the above boxes—it was simple, concise and to the point; there was no religious pretense; it was incredibly short—and shook the world around him. Take a look:

As Jesus was walking along, he saw a man who had been blind from birth. 'Rabbi,' his disciples asked him, 'why was this man born blind? Was it because of his own sins or his parents' sins?'

'It was not because of his sins or his parents' sins,' Jesus answered. 'This happened so the power of God could be seen in him. We must quickly carry out the tasks assigned us by the one who

sent us. The night is coming, and then no one can work. But while I am here in the world, I am the light of the world.'

Then he spit on the ground, made mud with the saliva, and spread the mud over the blind man's eyes. He told him, 'Go wash yourself in the pool of Siloam.' So the man went and washed and came back seeing!

His neighbors and others who knew him as a blind beggar asked each other, 'Isn't this the man who used to sit and beg?' Some said he was, and others said, 'No, he just looks like him!'

But the beggar kept saying, 'Yes, I am the same one!'

They asked, 'Who healed you? What happened?'

He told them, 'The man they call Jesus made mud and spread it over my eyes and told me, 'Go to the pool of Siloam and wash yourself.' So I went and washed, and now I can see!'

'Where is he now?' they asked.

'I don't know,' he replied.

Then they took the man who had been blind to the Pharisees, because it was on the Sabbath that Jesus had made the mud and healed him. The Pharisees asked the man all about it. So he told them, 'He put the mud over my eyes, and when I washed it away, I could see!'

Some of the Pharisees said, 'This man Jesus is not from God, for he is working on the Sabbath.' Others said, 'But how could an ordinary sinner do such miraculous signs?' So there was a deep division of opinion among them.

Then the Pharisees again questioned the man who had been blind and demanded, 'What's your opinion about this man who healed you?'

The man replied, 'I think he must be a prophet.'

The Jewish leaders still refused to believe the man had been blind and could now see, so they called in his parents. They asked them, 'Is this your son? Was he born blind? If so, how can he now see?'

His parents replied, 'We know this is our son and that he was born blind, but we don't know how he can see or who healed him. Ask him. He is old enough to speak for himself.' His parents said this because they were afraid of the Jewish leaders, who had announced that anyone saying Jesus was the Messiah would be expelled from the synagogue. That's why they said, 'He is old enough. Ask him.'

So for the second time they called in the man who had been blind and told him, 'God should get *the glory for this, because we know this man Jesus is a sinner.'*

'I don't know whether he is a sinner,' the man replied. 'But I know this: I was blind, and now I can see!'

John 9:1-25

Now I Can See!

When the blind man woke up on the morning of his healing, he had no idea that by the end of the day he would be able to see. But God came into his life, transformed his circumstances, put him on a new path and gave him a story to tell—a story that is still resonating with those who read and hear it over two thousand years later. Because the blind man was willing and eager to share the simple story of what Jesus had done in his life, he became a major Difference Maker for God.

Your story is a powerful tool that God will use to lead others to faith in him.

If you are a follower of Jesus, you have a story just as powerful as the blind man's. At one time, you were spiritually blind and God gave you eyes to see. The details of that transformation are as unique to you as your fingerprints, but when you are willing to share them with others who need Jesus, they carry incredible, relatable significance.

The blind man's story underscores three key truths about your own. First, your story is inarguable. No one can quibble over the details of what God has done in your life. Second, your story is interesting. The people in your life will want to hear it. Finally, your story is an investment in God's kingdom. As you attempt to influence others by telling it, God will multiply your efforts and use it to lead people to faith in him.

Inarguable: *No one can argue with what God has done in your life.*

The blind man's healing sparked a lot of questions. People who had known him all of his life were surprised by his sudden turnaround. They marveled, "Is this the same man we've seen begging?" The skeptics were quick to accuse Jesus of being something he wasn't and to try to discredit him. But no matter what questions or accusations were thrown up, the grateful man simply repeated his story. He didn't have all the answers, but he told his listeners what he knew: *I know this, I was blind, and now I can see!* (John 9:25)

No one can argue with what God has done in your life. Period. Your story is your story. The details of your own experiences can't be questioned. This truth leads to a lot of freedom. It relieves the self-imposed pressure of needing to know all the answers. When you have a personal story to tell, you don't have to know everything. You don't have to be able to address all of the *whys* and *hows*. All you have to know is what Jesus has done for you. All you have to do is tell your story simply and with the passion it deserves. God will do the rest.

I'm sure you've found yourself in gatherings of family or friends with someone who is skeptical about your faith. Maybe they make snide remarks about Christianity, without saying anything to you directly. Or maybe they pelt you with tough questions about the Bible, trying to undermine its validity. Situations like these make it easy to get quiet about your faith. You may feel like you aren't smart enough or prepared enough to answer the critics' questions. You're afraid they will hit you with something you don't know how to respond to. And maybe they will. But your story trumps anything and everything they may try to sling your way.

Keeping conversations focused on the specifics of your experience with Jesus cause the details that others may want to quibble over to fade into the background. When you are hit with a historical or theological question you don't know the answer to, a simple "I don't know about that, but let me tell you what Jesus has done for me," overrides it every time. Plus, the story of how Jesus has changed your life is what connects with people on an emotional level. It's the very thing that draws them in and changes the way they think—not the historical data and details they would like to focus on in an attempt to sidestep issues of the heart.

Interesting: *The people in your life will be interested in your story.*

When you share your story with the people in your life, you'll get many different responses. Some will be led closer to faith in Jesus. Others will stand back, surprised that you're a Christian. Some will be skeptical. Others will be curious about getting to know Jesus for themselves. But no matter how they respond, they'll all have one thing in common—they will be interested in the story you have to tell.

Your story has the ability to touch the people around you in a unique way simply because of your connection with them. They care about you. As such, they'll care about what is going on in your life—just as you care about what's going on in theirs. Their eyes may glaze over when there's a discussion about the Bible, or when they hear someone they don't know talking about God, but your story about what Jesus has done in you, for you and through you is guaranteed to make them tune in.

Your God story shifts theological conversations away from conjecture and makes the discussion personal. When you tell it humbly and authentically, others don't feel like you are trying to convince them of anything. You are simply relaying the truth as you have experienced it in your own life. Anyone who knows you personally won't be able to help but be interested in what you are saying.

Investment: *God will multiply your efforts to connect with others.*

Because of the blind man's eagerness to tell his simple story, people are still being touched today. He didn't know that his willingness to share his experience would end up changing countless lives. He didn't know that what happened to him would be used to shine the glory of God for generations to come. All he knew was that he was blind, he met Jesus, and then he could see. All he did was convey that story with enthusiasm. God took it from there. God multiplied the man's efforts so exponentially that you just read his story thousands of years later, thousands of miles away, in a different language than it was first recorded. That blind man never would have been able to comprehend such a reality.

You have no idea what God will do with your story as you begin to tell it. But you can rest assured that he will do something. He will use your story for his glory every single time it leaves your lips. Each time you mention something that God has done in your life, he will magnify that testimony. He will grow it. He will cause it to have influence with people who will then have influence with other people. Your simple story—the story you tend to discredit; the story you may be hesitant to tell because of misdirected fear—can truly have history- and eternity-changing effects.

Just stop and think for a minute: What if the blind man had been more like you and I tend to be? What if he had thought, "Maybe I shouldn't say anything about Jesus. Someone might think I'm a fanatic." Or what if he had reasoned, "I don't want to be lumped in with those other crazy Christians, so I'll just keep quiet." If he had let apprehension and doubt get the best of him, as we are so apt to do, then God's miraculous grace in his life would have been futile. Sure, he would have had his eyesight, but the truth of his experience wouldn't have touched anyone, changed any lives, or brought any glory to the one to whom he owed everything.

God has given you a story precisely so that you can tell it. Consider these words from scripture:

But God had mercy on me so that Christ Jesus could use me as a prime example of his great patience with even the worst sinners. Then others will real-ize that they, too, can believe in him and receive eternal life. (1 Timothy 1:16)

God has done magnificent work in your life so he can use you as an example to help others believe. Don't undermine his purposes by keeping your story to your-self. Tell it every chance you get. Who knows? He might still be using it to change the world long after you've gone to be with him in heaven.

4

the power of everyday moments

Success occurs when opportunity meets preparation.

Zig Ziglar

You encounter opportunities to be a Difference Maker every single day. God gives you chances to extend an invitation to church. He gives you openings to tell your story. He puts you in situations where he can use you to influence others, whether those others happen to be in your office, in your classroom, at the gym or around your dinner table. The problem isn't a lack of opportunity. The problem is that when an opportunity presents itself, you're not quite ready. Consider these scenarios:

- One of your coworkers tells you that she and her husband are heading toward a divorce. According to her, there's no hope for the relationship.

- While at dinner with a new friend who isn't a believer, there's an awkward pause when the food arrives because you want to pray… but you aren't sure how your friend will respond.

- A classmate sees you reading your small group book and asks you about it.

- An acquaintance mentions that his father has just received some devastating medical news and confides that the family is having a hard time dealing with what's to come.

- You're chitchatting with a neighbor at local coffee shop when she brings up something negative about an outspoken Christian who has been in the news.

Have you found yourself in situations similar to these? Situations where you know you should bring up your faith in Jesus, but you hesitate because you don't know what to say? God brings these divine appointments into your life so you can shine the light toward him, but if you aren't prepared to take advantage of them, they'll slip right by. The person you had the chance to influence will go on about his or her day, oblivious to the fact that he or she can share the hope you have in Jesus—and God won't get the glory he deserves in your life or in theirs.

Be prepared for the everyday moments of opportunity God brings your way.

The key to being a Difference Maker is to be prepared for the everyday moments of opportunity God brings your way. So far we've talked about two important ways you can take advantage of those opportunities. First, you can offer the person you're talking with an invitation to come to church with you (chapter 1). Second, you can share your personal God story (chapters 2 and 3).

In the pages ahead, you'll discover four more ways you can talk to the unbelievers in your life about the goodness of God. No matter what path you take to a conversation about your faith, you have to be ready to engage when you have the chance. You have to be aware of the opportunities around you and know when and how to take advantage of them.

Preparing to Make a Difference

You may have heard the old saying, "Seventy percent of success in life is just showing up." When it comes to being prepared to make a difference for God, you have to show up for him in three ways: physically, spiritually, and intellectually. In other words:

- Be where God wants you to be.
  (Physical Readiness)

- Be aware of who God wants you to invest in. (Spiritual Readiness)

- Be prepared to share your faith.
  (Intellectual Readiness)

Each of these three areas of preparedness is essential to being a Difference Maker.

Physical Readiness

Being physically ready to make a difference is as simple as being where God wants you to be. You can't influence anyone if you aren't there for the divine appointments he has in store. If you are walking with God, following his lead in your life, then you have been placed exactly where you are supposed to be. He has led you to the city you are living in. He has you in your current workplace for a reason. He has put you in the neighborhood you're in so you can represent him.

In all of those places, every day of your life, show up for God. Be where you should be so he can use you in the ways he wants to. Be willing to connect with other people. Only then will you have the opportunity to invite them to church. Only then will you get the chance to tell them your story. It's only when you are willing to be physically present in the places God has called you to that you will be able to take advantage of the divine appointments he has set up for you.

Spiritual Readiness

God is at work in the lives of the people around you. Your best opportunity for influence comes as you become aware of the ways he's working and then join him in that work. Be sensitive to who God would have you invest in. He's already positioning them to be open to your touch.

You will cross paths with two types of unbelievers: (1) those who are skeptical of Christianity and seem closed to the idea of God; and (2) those who are not yet followers of Jesus but who are more open. The people in your life who ask you questions about God from time to time, or make small comments indicating they are wrestling with the concept of faith, fall into this second category. They may not say it, but they are searching. As Henry Blackaby wrote in *Experiencing God*:

> *People don't ask questions about spiritual matters unless God is at work in their lives. When you see someone seeking God or asking questions about Christianity, you are witnessing God at work.*[3]

One of the mistakes you and I most often make is that we become so concerned with the hard cases around us that we miss those more discreet family members, friends and acquaintances desperately in need of God's love. We miss those who would be open if only we would engage them in conversation.

There are three times in life when people tend to be most receptive to the gospel—when they are under tension, undergoing transition, or in trouble. These three states help people catch a glimpse of the bigger picture. Thanks to the flickering realization that they can't control everything or handle every aspect of life on their own, they begin to see their need for God.

As you think about the people in your life, who do you know that's under tension undergoing transition, or in trouble? Think about what those you love are going through. Has anyone just moved? Changed jobs? Had a new baby? Do you know someone who has relational problems in her family? Or who is facing financial hardship? Is anyone dealing with an addiction or an ongoing physical ailment? Staying aware of what's going on in the lives of the people God has put around you will help you be prepared to share your faith with them when they are most receptive to hearing it.

Intellectual Readiness

Imagine that tomorrow afternoon, you are where you're supposed to be. You're chatting with one of the people God has uniquely positioned in your life. And then, all of a sudden, an opportunity to talk about your faith presents itself. You see your opening. What do you do?

First, you have to do a quick mental evaluation of the scenario. Would this be a good time for an invitation to church? Or is this your chance to share your story? After having worked through the first few chapters of this book, you should be intellectually prepared to do either one of those things. When you choose one of these two approaches, make sure to tailor what you say to the person you are talking to as much as possible. If you tell your story, again, emphasize the parts you think the person you're talking with may be able to best relate to. If you are offering a simple invitation to church and you know the person you are talking to likes tacos, say, "Why don't you come to church with me Sunday morning and we'll grab some tacos after?" You get the point. Don't be canned. Be personal.

While extending an invitation to church and sharing your personal story are two of the best, easiest ways to be a Difference Maker, sometimes God will put you in situations where you have the opportunity to go even further. Every once in a while, he will send someone your way who is desperately seeking his truth—someone who turns to you, asking heartfelt questions about what it means to be a Christian, searching for an explanation of faith that makes sense to them. If God were to bring that kind of divine appointment into your life, would you know what to say? Would you be ready?

Four Illustrations of Faith

In the chapters ahead, I am going to give you four simple ways to communicate what it means to be a follower of Jesus. These are four illustrations that will help you share the basics of your faith. Think of them as tools in a toolbox. You should be familiar with how and when to use each one, so you can pull the right tool out no matter what situation you find yourself in. They are:

- ***The Bridge***—This simple illustration will help you convey how Jesus bridges the gap between God and his creation.

- ***Do vs. Done***—Many of the people in your life feel like they have to work for God's love. This illustration dispels that myth.

- ***The Morality Ladder***—Know anyone who thinks being a good person is enough to get into heaven? This illustration will help you explain why that reasoning is flawed.

- ***The Romans Road***—This straightforward approach to the gospel gives you a way to use God's own words to outline the path from sin to salvation for anyone wondering what Christianity is all about.

As you study how to use each of these approaches, pay attention to which one feels the most natural to you. That's the one you'll be most comfortable using as you talk with others. But even as you make one of these your go-to, familiarize yourself with all of them. Part of being intellectually prepared to share your faith is being able to quickly choose the best tool for whatever situation you find yourself in and to know how to use it well.

Everyday Preparation

A professor friend of mine recently told me about a conversation she'd had with a young lady in one of her classes, Sara. Sara was a good overall student, but a terrible test-taker. She always sabotaged herself in two ways. First, she put too much pressure on herself to perform when the time came. Second, she didn't know how to prepare for tests well. The unfortunate combination not only left her with a lot of anxiety on test days, but it also all-but-guaranteed that she wouldn't do well.

After Sara had done poorly on yet another test she should have aced, my friend pulled her aside and got her talking about the problem. Sara admitted that not feeling prepared was her biggest downfall. If only she were better prepared when the test came, she wouldn't have so much anxiety. My friend gave Sara some study tips and assured her that a little quality preparation would go a long way in helping her answer each question with confidence.

As my friend told me about Sara, I couldn't help but see the similarities between Sara's problem and our own hesitancy to share our faith. Most of us get nervous talking to others about Jesus because we don't feel prepared. So when our moment comes, we miss it or mess it up. But, if you and I want to be Difference Makers, we don't have the luxury of walking around unprepared for the questions we might face. The stakes are too high.

The everyday opportunities you and I need to prepare for are much more important than an academic exam. The moments God gives us for influence impact real lives and real eternities. This is something Paul understood as he was writing to the Christians in Ephesus with this request:

> *Ask God to give me the right words so I can boldly explain God's mysterious plan that the Good News is for Jews and Gentiles alike.* (Ephesians 6:19)

I pray that as you study the next four chapters, you will be filled with a sense of the spiritual urgency that surrounds your calling to be prepared to share Jesus with people in your life. As you familiarize yourself with the following illustrations, do so knowing that you can be confident in your ability to speak with boldness and love when God presents you with a divine appointment.

5

preparing to make a difference
the bridge

I tell you the truth, those who listen to my message and believe in God who sent me have eternal life. They will never be condemned for their sins, but they have already passed from death into life.

Jesus (John 5:24)

Imagine you are sitting at lunch or over a cup of coffee with a friend when the conversation turns toward faith. Maybe your friend confesses that he has never truly understood the fundamentals of Christianity. He admits to being so distracted by how the Christian faith is portrayed in culture that he has never paid much attention to what it means to need Jesus. Like so many

71

others, he assumes that Jesus was a great teacher or a prophet but nothing more. Or maybe your friend argues that Christianity works for some people, but he doesn't see why it should be considered better or truer than any other religion. Enter the bridge illustration.

Before we dive into the bridge, here are a few things to keep in mind about this illustration and the ones I'll cover in the following three chapters:

- As I detail these illustrations, I will do so with language you might want to use as you share with the people God puts in your path. But I am not giving you a script. Take what's foundational and make it your own.

- One of the best things about these illustrations is that you can keep them extremely casual and conversational. Simply jot the needed visuals down on a napkin or a scrap of paper while you talk. *I'll explain how to do this in italics, throughout.* These visual representations of Christianity's core message will stick with people for a long time.

• Once you have talked through one of these illustrations with someone, your best next step will usually be to invite that person to church with you. Occasionally, though, you may find yourself with someone who wants to repent and accept salvation on the spot. When that happens, simply pray a prayer with your friend along the lines of the one detailed at the end of this chapter. Then refer this brand new believer to your pastor and/ or invite him or her to join you at the next church service.

Building The Bridge

Have you ever wrestled with a sense of emptiness? Most people have. At some point in life, we all become aware of a longing in our hearts that nothing in the world seems to fill. Many have described this longing as a God-shaped hole within us—a hole that is the result of the separation between God and us.

As you are talking, grab a piece of paper or a napkin and sketch two simple cliffs. Write 'You and Me' on one cliff and 'God' on the other:

73

Fig. 1: Bridge step one

The separation that exists between you and me and God is the result of sin. Many people are confused by what sin is, but it's simple. Sin is the act of stepping outside of God's best plan for our lives. It's when we know what God says to do, but we decide to do our own thing instead. We are all guilty of sin. No human being is perfect. But God is perfect, which is why our sin creates a chasm between him and us. Sin separates us from his peace, his presence and his power. If we die without solving our sin problem, we will be separated from him for eternity.

Since the beginning of time, various philosophies and faith systems have been trying to answer the question, "How do we overcome the separation between us and God?" Many people think they can close the chasm by being a good person. They try to build a bridge of good works. Others subscribe to religious routines and rituals, hoping their efforts will please God enough to get across. And many simply ignore the two cliffs and try to fill their emptiness in other ways. They throw themselves into climbing the corporate ladder, planning never-ending family activities, engaging in unhealthy relationships, or even abusing drugs or alcohol. Anything can serve as a distraction for a while—but the separation is still there.

Scripture teaches that there's only one way to bridge the gap between us and God. That's by accepting the gift of salvation he offers through his son, Jesus. Knowing you and I would never be able to reach him through our own efforts, God sent Jesus to act as our intermediary. Jesus came to earth, lived a perfect life, and died a criminal's death on the cross as a sacrifice for every sin you and I have ever committed and will ever commit. *Around this point, roughly sketch a cross connecting the two cliffs and write Jesus on it.*

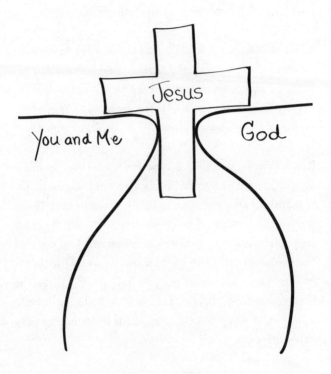

Fig. 2: Bridge step two

The cross bridges the gap of separation caused by sin, making it possible for us to get from where we are to where God is. When we accept its message, we can move into God's presence. Jesus himself said:

> I tell you the truth, those who listen to my message and believe in God who sent me have eternal life. They will never be condemned for their sins, but they have already **passed from death into life**.
>
> (John 5:24, emphasis added)

If you've never put your trust in Jesus, you have a choice to make. Will you cross the bridge God has built for you and pass from death to life? Or will you keep living separated from him, filled with emptiness and longing? Jesus offers not only the promise of eternal life, but also the promise of a better life here and now—a life that is in line with God's best. All you have to do is take the first step onto the bridge. He has already done the rest.

If you're ready to place your faith in Jesus, just pray this simple prayer:

> Dear God, I open my heart to you and invite you into my life. I confess that I am a sinner. I ask that you would forgive me of all that I've done wrong. Thank you for sending your Son, Jesus, who died

for me and who gives me the opportunity to know you. From this moment on, I want to follow Jesus, in the fellowship of his church. Thank you for accepting me. In Jesus' name I pray. Amen.

6

preparing to make a difference
do vs. done

There's nothing more. There's never less.
There's only you, and I am blessed.
It's already been done.

Rush of Fools

Many of the unbelievers in your sphere of influence share a common misconception about
Christianity. Namely, they believe that Christianity has
too many requirements; that there's a to-do list and a
not-to-do list, neither of which they want to get on
board with. This line of thinking is widespread because
most people see Christianity as a religion, and most

people spell religion DO. *As you talk, jot down the following equation:*

$$Religion = \mathbf{DO}$$

The majority of world religions are about people trying to work their way to God. In one form or another, they advocate following set rules and adhering to specific rituals in an attempt to win approval from a higher power. But in that regard, Christianity is not a religion at all. In fact, it's the antithesis of religion. Rather than being about what we do to earn God's favor, it's about who we are in Jesus Christ.

Unfortunately, since Christianity is so often lumped in with conventional religions, it's easy for an emphasis on ritual, self-effort and works to seep into our understanding of the faith and create confusion. But while religion is effort-centered, Christianity is grace-centered. Christian belief hinges on what God has done to show his love for us and secure our right standing with him, rather than what we can do to earn it. *Jot down the following equation underneath the first:*

$$Christianity = \mathbf{DONE}$$

A Cultural Problem

Those of us raised with a western mindset are quick to fall into DO rather than DONE thinking. We have been brought up with a do-it-yourself mentality. As self-sufficient Americans, we operate in the realm of cause and effect—what we do determines what we get. If we don't have what we need, we're told to pull ourselves up by our bootstraps and go after it harder. We think that if we control the variables, we can control the outcome. While this may be a great attitude to have in many other areas of life, it is not true with God. As one insightful author notes:

> *The great crisis of the churchgoer is that his action does not save him. He must base his faith on someone outside his control. He cannot make Christ redeem him, or manipulate Christ into redeeming him. He can only trust Christ.*[4]

In Christianity, there is only one action we have to take to bring ourselves into right standing with God, and that is to choose a heartfelt relationship with Jesus. When we recognize the truth of Jesus' message, we have to give up our perceived ability to control God through rules and rituals and, instead, hand ourselves over to his grace. Jesus himself tells us:

83

No one can come to the Father except through me.
(John 14:6)

These words leave no choice but to let go of the false
security of religious activity, and recognize that Jesus—
and no one or nothing else—is our source of salvation.
Add to that these words from the Apostle Paul:

*God saved you by his grace when you believed.
And you can't take credit for this; it is a gift from
God.* (Ephesians 2:8-9)

There is nothing you and I can do to earn our way to
God; it has already been done. Remember:

Religion = **DO**
Christianity = **DONE**

Motivation Matters

While it may not be necessary to go any further when
using this illustration, it is worth thinking through the
issue of what motivates right actions. Take the following
for your own knowledge, or in case the person you are
sharing with has questions along these lines.

Being in a relationship with Jesus puts you in right
standing with God—there's no other action you need to

take to assure his approval and your salvation—but that doesn't mean you stop taking right actions. Rather, your motivation changes. You and I instinctively understand this truth when it comes to our human relationships. When we are in a healthy relationship, we treat the other person with respect. We do things to please, rather than to hurt or offend. We aren't trying to win approval anymore; we are simply operating within the positive overflow of a good connection. Right actions are the natural result of a right, loving relationship.

Here's the tricky part. Right actions alone do not necessarily indicate a right relationship. It's all too possible to do the right things for the wrong reasons. Religious thinking purports that if you do the right things, a relationship with God will follow. But, again, religion has it backwards. Instead, a healthy relationship with God should motivate you toward right actions done out of love, not obligation. There is no to-do or not-to-do list that will suck the fun out of life; there is only a new, better way of living steeped in the truth and joy of a loving relationship with the one who created you.

7

preparing to make a difference
the morality ladder

The word 'gospel' means 'good news.' The good news is that good people don't go to heaven—forgiven people do.

Andy Stanley

If you were to ask a cross-section of people on the street whether they're going to go to heaven when they die, the most common response you'd get would be something along the lines of, "I hope so. I've always tried to be a good person." Good Person Theology, as I like to call it, is our culture's predominant theology. Studies show eighty percent of Americans buy into it. The thinking is that there is some sort of invisible morality ladder leaned up against the wall to heaven. The better you are, the higher you climb. If you die having done more good than bad, then you've probably made it high enough to walk through the pearly gates.

Whenever you find yourself in conversation with someone who subscribes to Good Person Theology, try engaging him or her in a little interactive game. Grab a piece of paper and *sketch a ladder*. Write *Good/Heaven* at the top of the ladder and *Bad/Hell* at the bottom of the ladder. Then, have a little fun asking your friend to place some people on the ladder. First have them give you the names of a few "bad people" who might be at the bottom. They may say Hitler, Charles Manson, or even someone they know personally. Then prompt them to put some people at the very top of the ladder. They're likely to offer up names like Mother Theresa or Martin Luther King, Jr. *Write the names they come up with on the ladder.*

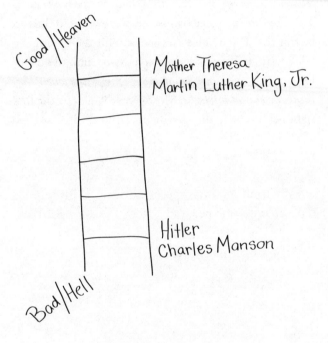

Fig. 3: Morality Ladder step one

Finally, ask them to put themselves on the morality ladder. *Hand them the pen and have them write 'me' at whatever level of the ladder they think they've made it to.* They'll probably place themselves somewhere in the top half of the sketch. This is when you hit them with the big question: How high do you have to climb to qualify for heaven? *Have them point out or draw a line where they think the cut-off might be.* Most people will draw the line right below where they see themselves.

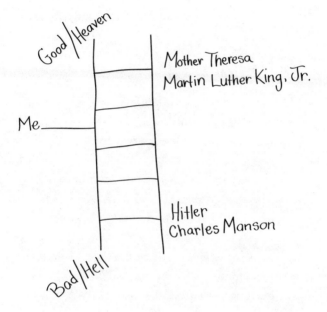

Fig. 4: Morality Ladder step two

With Good Person Theology, everyone likes to think they've done just enough to make it into heaven, but there's always an underlying anxiety ... because maybe they haven't. There's no assurance they're going to make the cut.

A Rickety Ladder, At Best

When you examine it a little more closely, there are a lot of holes in the morality ladder and the Good Person Theology it's based on. Here are two of the biggest:

1. There's no clear, agreed-upon definition of what a good person is. Different people believe it to be different things.

2. Jesus' teaching directly contradicts the premise behind this entire line of reasoning. As one author writes, "Jesus assured the most religious people of his day that they weren't good enough to enter God's kingdom, while promising criminals and prostitutes that God would gladly welcome them."[5] Anyone who places value on what Jesus said (and most people who buy in to the morality ladder do) would be hard pressed to reconcile his words with Good Person Theology.

The truth is, there is no such thing as being good enough to get into heaven. You can't climb high enough on the morality ladder. No matter what rung you think you've ascended to, you aren't good enough to make the cut and you never will be—on your own, that is. Because God is perfect, the requirement for joining him in eternity is perfection. None of us can achieve that perfection by trying harder or scaling higher (Romans 3:10).

The great scandal of Christianity is that God offers his grace freely to anyone and everyone who believes in his son, Jesus. Because of grace, our pasts—whether glowing or grotesque—have no bearing on whether we can enter into a relationship with God, enjoy him in the present and spend eternity with him in heaven. Thanks to Jesus' perfect life and his sacrifice for us on the cross, we can toss the rickety old morality ladder to the side, knowing that we are made right with God through faith rather than effort. *Draw an 'X' through the morality ladder and then draw a line connecting 'Me' to 'Good/Heaven.' Write 'Grace' beside that line.*

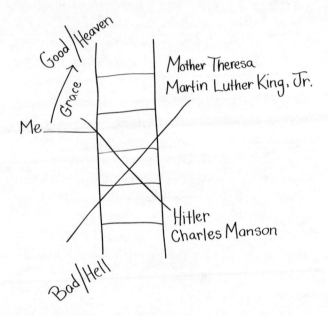

Fig. 5: Morality Ladder step three

As the Apostle Paul wrote:

> *We are made right with God by placing our faith in Jesus Christ. And this is true for everyone who believes, no matter who we are.* (Romans 3:22)

Freedom is found in rejecting human-made morality systems and choosing instead to accept Jesus' love. When you place your faith in him, his grace will cover you. You don't have to live in uncertainty, continually trying to earn some elusive approval. You don't have to hope you'll go to heaven when you die. You can live with the assurance that, because of your faith, you will spend eternity with God. Stop trusting in your own goodness, and relax into the free gift of forgiveness.

8

preparing to make a difference
romans road

For 'Everyone who calls on the name of the Lord will be saved.'
Apostle Paul (Romans 10:13)

Close to sixty years after Jesus' crucifixion, the Apostle Paul wrote a letter to guide and encourage the Christians in Rome. According to many scholars, this letter—which we know as the book of Romans— offers the clearest presentation of Christian doctrine in the entire Bible. Nestled within its pages, Paul gives us a handful of verses that perfectly outline the concept of sin and salvation. Like a how-to guide for understanding Christianity, these verses work together to illustrate the basics of the gospel message and explain what we need to do to be saved. Take a look:

Romans 3:23—For everyone has sinned; we all fall short of God's glorious standard.

Romans 6:23—For the wages of sin is death, but the free gift of God is eternal life through Christ Jesus our Lord.

Romans 5:8—But God showed his great love for us by sending Christ to die for us while we were still sinners.

Romans 10:9-10—If you openly declare that Jesus is Lord and believe in your heart that God raised him from the dead, you will be saved. For it is by believing in your heart that you are made right with God, and it is by openly declaring your faith that you are saved.

Romans 10:13—For "Everyone who calls on the name of the Lord will be saved."

These verses, taken together, are often referred to as the Romans Road to salvation. The Romans Road is a great tool to use when you're in a conversation about faith with someone who doesn't understand Christianity or who questions the need for Jesus. By simply presenting each verse, you can let Paul do the talking for you.

The Road to Salvation

Think of the individual Romans Road verses as a series of guideposts. Each verse serves as a marker along the road, directing the conversation and keeping it focused on biblical truth. Start at Guidepost One.

Guidepost One—Romans 3:23

For everyone has sinned; we all fall short of God's glorious standard.

Paul offers a clear reminder that every living human being has sinned. Not one of us can live up to God's standard of holiness through our own effort, as we discussed in the morality ladder illustration (chapter 7). By its very nature, the sin that exists in your life and mine separates us from God.

Guidepost Two—Romans 6:23

For the wages of sin is death, but the free gift of God is eternal life through Christ Jesus our Lord.

Sin carries a hefty penalty: death. Not only is physical death the result of sin, but eternal death, as well. When you die without knowing Jesus, you die to the possibility of spending eternity with God in heaven. But, the good news of the gospel is that God has given us a way to conquer death. He loves you and me so much that he sent his son to pay the wages of our sin.

Guidepost Three—Romans 5:8

But God showed his great love for us by sending Christ to die for us while we were still sinners.

God didn't wait for you and me to clean up our act. While we were still steeped in sin, he provided a way for us to be brought into a right relationship with him. He sent his son to die in our place. Three days after Jesus was crucified, he rose from the grave. His death and resurrection are the lynchpin of the Christian faith.

Guidepost Four—Romans 10:9-10

If you openly declare that Jesus is Lord and believe in your heart that God raised him from the dead, you will be saved. For it is by believing in your heart that you are made right with God, and it is by openly declaring your faith that you are saved.

All you have to do to accept the gift of salvation is believe in your heart that Jesus is the Son of God and confess that belief with your mouth. In other words, ask him to come into your life, forgive you and be your Lord. If you've never done that, simply pray a prayer like this:

Dear God, I open my heart to you and invite you into my life. I confess that I am a sinner. I ask that you would forgive me of all that I've done wrong. Thank you for sending your Son, Jesus, who died for me and who gives me the opportunity to know you. From this moment on, I want to follow Jesus, in the fellowship of his church. Thank you for accepting me. In Jesus' name I pray. Amen.

When you accept Jesus as your savior, you can know that your sins have been forgiven and that you will go to heaven when you die.

Guidepost Five—Romans 10:13
For "Everyone who calls on the name of the Lord will be saved."

No matter who you are or what you've done (or not done) in the past, God's promises are for you. If you understand the truths revealed by the five guideposts along the Romans Road, and if you act on them by placing your faith in Jesus, you will receive God's incredible gift of salvation; you will experience a level of living in this world that is only possible when you are under the umbrella of his blessing; and you will be able to face the rest of your days knowing that your eternity in heaven is secure.

9

are you willing?

*[Jesus] knew who he was. He knew where he had come from,
and why he was here. And he knew where he was going. And
when you are that liberated, then you can serve.*

Howard Hendricks

As you think back over your journey of faith, I bet
someone who influenced you greatly comes to
mind. Maybe it was a friend who invited you to church
for the first time. Perhaps it was a parent or grandparent
who was intentional about sharing the things of God
with you. Or it could have been a co-worker, classmate
or neighbor who was quick to tell her God story whenever given the opportunity. Someone was a Difference
Maker in your life. Who was it?

Without that person, your story might look completely different than it does right now. If not for your Difference Maker's influence, you could still be adrift, missing out on the life God is blessing you with, and wrestling with uncertainty about eternity. But because someone was willing to take a step toward you, your present and your future were forever impacted for the better.

Willing to Make a Difference

Here's one thing I can guarantee about the person who influenced you for God: doing so required leaving his or her comfort zone. Making a difference usually does. Depending on the circumstances and the relationship, your Difference Maker may have only had to take a small step away from comfort—or he may have had to take a huge leap. He may have been afraid of what you would think of him. He may have feared you would project negative perceptions about Christianity onto him. He may have worried you'd think he was crazy if he told you his story, or that you'd whisper behind his back if he invited you to church.

But he did it anyway. At some point, the person who made a difference in your life acknowledged that all of these fears were whispers and lies of the enemy, trying to keep him quiet. He realized that there was no reason to be timid about his faith. He became willing to step out of his comfort zone and toward you. Aren't you glad?

Because someone was willing to take a step toward you, your present and your future were forever impacted for the better.

Putting yourself out there always requires a little discomfort. There's some sacrifice involved in every non-routine interaction. After all, every one of us could choose to put our blinders on and go through the motions of daily living, oblivious to anything outside our own little circle of concern. That may be comfortable for a while, but we would be of no use to anyone. After a time, we wouldn't even be of use to ourselves. To live well is to venture something. To live in a way that intentionally impacts other people's lives is to venture even more. And to be willing to be a Difference Maker is to venture greatly.

The Ultimate Difference Maker

Whenever I become tentative about talking one-on-one with a friend, family member or acquaintance about Jesus (and believe me, I still do!), I simply remind myself of how Jesus stepped out of his comfort zone for me.

Imagine what was going on in Jesus' mind and heart the night before he was crucified. While he knew that the events unfolding were God's plan, he was in anguish over the prospect of being mocked, abused and nailed to a cross to die. In fact, just hours before his death, Jesus knelt in the Garden of Gethsemane and begged his Father:

> *'My Father! If it is possible, let this cup of suffering be taken away from me...'* (Matthew 26:39)

Having become so accustomed to the story of Jesus' crucifixion, it's all-too-easy for you and me to dismiss the struggle going on inside him during those final hours. Jesus was every bit as human as he was deity. While he wanted to fulfill the purpose he had been put on earth for, he dreaded the pain and suffering it would take. Still, Jesus was willing to endure—willing to be uncomfortable to the point of death—to be the Difference Maker for you, for me, and for every person who has ever lived. As he went on to say that night in the garden:

> *'...Yet I want your will to be done, not mine.'*
> (Matthew 26:39)

Even though Jesus experienced every temptation you and I have ever experienced, he never gave in. I'm sure he was tempted to stay quiet some days. He may not have felt like engaging the crowds every time they gathered. When he came face-to-face with people who were critical of God's message, he may have wanted to downshift into small talk about the weather in Jerusalem. But God had called him to a higher purpose—a purpose he fulfilled with humility and grace.

Jesus was the ultimate Difference Maker. He was ready to do whatever it took to reconcile us to his Father. He was willing to die so that we could have the opportunity to live our earthly lives in step with God before spending eternity in heaven. As such, how could you and I be anything but willing to offer his good news to others?

Are You Willing?

God has uniquely positioned you to influence the people in your life for him. He wants to use you. He wants to partner with you in changing lives and eternities. And he only has one requirement you have to meet in order to qualify: You simply have to be willing to participate. You have to be open to using your everyday life for eternal impact. God is calling you to make a difference. Are you willing?

appendix a
resources for further study

For more on…

- Sharing your story, see:
  Becoming a Contagious Christian by Bill Hybels and Mark Mittelberg

- The Bridge, see:
  Peace with God by Dr. Billy Graham

- Do vs. Done, see:
  The Case for Faith: A Journalist Investigates the Toughest Objections to Christianity by Lee Strobel

- The Morality Ladder, see:
  How Good is Good Enough? by Andy Stanley

appendix b
scripture guide

As you begin influencing your world as a Difference Maker, these verses can strengthen and support you when you are feeling…

Afraid:

Psalm 27:1, 5; 34:4; 56:1-13; 91:1-16; Isaiah 35:4; 41:10; John 14-27; Hebrews 13:6; 1 John 4:18

Angry:

Psalm 37:8; Proverbs 14:29; 15:1; Matthew 5:22-24; Romans 12:10-21; Ephesians 4:26, 31-32; James 1:19-20

Anxious/Worried:

Psalm 37:5; 46:1-11; 55:22; Proverbs 3:5-6;
Matthew 6:25-34; Philippians 4:6-7; 1 Peter 5:7

Bereaved:

Psalm 23; Isaiah 25:8; John 11:25; 14:1-3;
1 Corinthians 15:55; 2 Corinthians 5:1; Philippians 1:21;
1 Thessalonians 4:13-18; 1 Peter 1:3-4

Bitter/Resentful:

Matthew 6:14-15; Romans 12:14-15; 1 Peter 2:23

Depressed:

Psalm 27:13-14; 34:1-22; 42:1-11; Isaiah 41:10;
Matthew 11:28-30; Romans 8:28; Philippians 4:13

Discouraged/Disappointed:

Matthew 11:28-30; Romans 8:28; 2 Corinthians 4:8-9,
16-18; Galatians 6:9; Phillipians1:6; 4:6-7, 19;
1 Thessalonians 3:3; Hebrews 10:35-36; 1 Peter 1:6-9

Distraught/Upset:

Psalm 31:24; 61:1-2; 103:13-14; Luke 18:1-8;
Hebrews 12:3; 13:5; 1 Peter 5:7

Doubting:

John 6:37; 10:27-29; Philippians 1:6; 2 Timothy 1:12;
Hebrews 11:6; 12:2; 1 John 5:13

Far From God:

Psalm 139:1-18; Proverbs 28:13; Isaiah 55:7;
Lamentations 3:22-23; Luke 15:11-24;
Revelation 2:4-5

Jealous/Envious:

Exodus 20:17; Proverbs 14:30; 27:4; 1 Corinthians 3:3;
Galatians 5:19-21, 26; Hebrews 13:5; James 3:16; 5:9

Lonely:

Psalm 25:16-18; Isaiah 46:4; 55:12; John 14:15-21;
Acts 2:25-26; Hebrews 13:5-6

Sad:

Psalm 91:14-15; 119:50; Isaiah 43:2; 61:1-3;
2 Corinthians 1:3-4; 2 Thessalonians 2:16-17;
Hebrews 4:15-16

Sick:

Exodus 15:26; 23:25; Psalm 30:2; 41:3; 91:3-10;
103:3-5; 107:20; Jeremiah 30:17; 33:6; Matthew 9:35;
James 5:14-15; 3 John 2

Tempted:

Psalm 119:9-11; Matthew 4:1-4, 11;
1 Corinthians 10:12-13; James 1:2-3, 12-15; 4:7

Troubled By Wrong Thoughts:

Joshua 1:8; Psalm 1:1-6; 4:4; 19:7-14; Isaiah 26:3;
Philippians 4:8; Colossians 3:2

acknowledgments

Nelson Searcy: Thank you to Jesus Christ for being the difference maker in my life. Thank you to everyone who shared Christ with me as a teenager and to all who have helped me grow in Christ to this day. Thank you to Jennifer Dykes Henson for her ongoing and ever deepening commitment to our writing partnership. Thank you to Kerrick Thomas, Executive Pastor at The Journey, who originally co-taught many of the sermons on which this book is based. Thank you to the entire Church Leader Insights team, but especially Sandra Olivieri who shepherded this book into existence. Thank you to all the staff and members at The Journey Church. To my wife, Kelley, and son, Alexander (who turned 9 during the writing of this book and is one inch away from five feet tall), I could not do what I do without your unending love and support—thank you!

Jennifer Dykes Henson: Thanks first and foremost to God for inviting me to be involved in this important work. Thanks also to Nelson Searcy. The evolution of our partnership over the last 10 years continues to humble and amaze me. I'm honored to be completing another life-altering, eternity-changing book with you. Finally, thank you to my love and partner on this journey, Brian, and to our two baby girls, Isabelle and Ivey Grace. You three are the difference makers in my life, today and always.

notes

1. Various reports are done annually on this topic. Check online for the latest. For one early influential study, see www.lifeway.com/Article/LifeWay-Research-finds-Americans-open-to-outreach-from-churches

2. Niequist, Shauna. *Savor: Living Abundantly Where You Are, As You Are.* Grand Rapids: Zondervan, 2015.

3. Blackaby, Henry T., and Claude V. King. *Experiencing God: How to Live the Full Adventure of Knowing and Doing the Will of God.* Nashville: Broadman & Holman, 1994.

4. Miller, Donald. "Jesus Contends with Religion." *Storyline Blog*. Web. 1 June 2015.

5. Stanley, Andy. *How Good Is Good Enough?* Sisters, OR: Multnomah, 2003.

ABOUT NELSON SEARCY

 Nelson Searcy is the founding and lead pastor of The Journey Church, with locations in Manhattan, Queens, San Francisco and Boca Raton, where Nelson and his family reside. He is the author of over a dozen books, including *The Greatness Principle: Finding Significance and Joy in Serving Others* and *The Generosity Ladder: Your Next Step to Financial Peace*. Nelson and his church appear routinely on lists such as "The 50 Most Influential Churches" and "The 25 Most Innovative Leaders." As founder of ChurchLeaderInsights.com, he's trained more than 50,000 church leaders, with over 3,000 of them being church planters. His continued mission is to help church leaders and church members around the world cooperate with God to fulfill the Great Commission.

HOW TO HANDLE YOUR FINANCES IN A GODLY MANNER

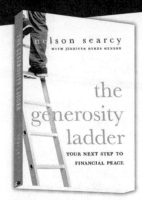

Published alongside *Maximize* is Searcy's book **The Generosity Ladder**, for anyone who desires to handle money with excellence. Written to answer all of the questions and misunderstandings that surround the intersection of God and money, *The Generosity Ladder* will allow laypeople to fully grasp God's plan for their finances.

Maximize is the ultimate how-to book for pastors and church leaders who long for their churches to be fully resourced and able to carry out ministry initiatives without financial strain. Shining a light on the often taboo subject of money, *Maximize* offers an innovative, step-by-step plan for systemizing and maximizing financial gifts while growing strong disciples.

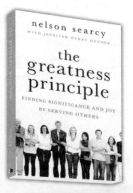

HOW TO LIVE EACH DAY WITH AN ATTITUDE OF WORSHIP

FOR CHURCH MEMBERS

With **Revolve**, readers will see that when they approach worship with a "what can I get out of this" attitude, they're bound to be disappointed. However, worshiping God as a way of life not only honors God but also satisfies our souls. Built-in action steps at the end of each short chapter will give readers specific ideas about how to refocus their attention on God and live each day in an attitude of worship.

FOR WORSHIP LEADERS

Engage, the church leaders' companion to *Revolve*, is a step-by-step, stress-free guide to planning worship services that allow for and foster true life change.

These books are available at Amazon.com and ChristianBook.com
For other resources, visit www.ChurchLeaderInsights.com